A Butler's Guide to
Table Manners

A Butler's Guide to
Table Manners

Nicholas Clayton

 THE NATIONAL TRUST

First published in the United Kingdom in 2007 by
National Trust Books
151 Freston Road
London
W10 6TH

An imprint of Anova Books Company Ltd

Designed by Lee-May Lim and Nichola Smith

Illustrations by Matt Windsor from original
references supplied by the author.

ISBN-13 9781905400485

A CIP catalogue record for this book is available from the British Library.

10 9 8 7 6 5 4 3 2 1

Printed and bound by MPG Books Ltd, Bodmin, UK

This book can be ordered direct from the publisher at the website:

www.anovabooks.com

Or try your local bookshop

For J D

CONTENTS

BASIC TRAINING

'He's a gentleman,' wrote George Bernard Shaw
about Henry Higgins in his preface to *Pygmalion*,
'Just look at his boots.'

A part from the borderline psychotic behaviour of one or two of the Masters at the Preparatory School for Boys that I attended in Hertfordshire in the early 1960s, most of the sentence I served remains a blur.

Impossible to forget is the emphasis that was put on manners. It was made abundantly clear to us, the inmates, that as well as having to be able to conjugate perfectly what we, at the time, considered utterly useless Latin, do algebra and spell words that we only understood the meaning of years later, we had to know how to behave in public and especially how to behave at the table; failure to do this led inevitably to Saturday mornings in detention.

Lunchtimes were more often than not a fiasco of semi-cooked food, some of which made excellent missiles. Matron had a severe nasal disorder so was never quite sure when to remove things from the oven; presumably she couldn't smell if the food was cooked or not. Once our lunch was plonked on our tables, anyone seen eating Matron's experiments in an inappropriate way was rapped over the knuckles with a length of timber by the duty officer, branded the dreadful name of guttersnipe, and 'invited' to a Saturday morning meeting.

Good manners were so high on the agenda that Mr B, our Burberry-clad headmaster, had signs made in six-inch lettering which he nailed up over the chalkboards with the heel of a riding boot. The signs read, 'Manners Maketh Man'. You couldn't miss them and they were quite useful to rest the eyes on during long periods of certain Masters' wild chalk scrawling, having abandoned all hope of deciphering anything, and in an attempt to avoid the onset of an afternoon nap.

Although my Latin is still weak and algebra a total mystery, I am very grateful for everything that I learned on Saturday mornings; the lessons have stood me in good stead over the years and have been a lot more use to me than algebra.

Mr B's signs over the chalkboards would not be considered 'politically correct' these days; however they were a constant reminder to us, and the adage still holds true today. 'How to behave' training ought to be part of The National Curriculum – after all, good manners cost nothing but are worth millions! Furthermore, learning to behave well did us no harm whatsoever, which is more than can be said for Matron's cooking!

Nicholas Clayton

MANNERS MAKETH MAN (AND WOMAN)

A comment in a leading national newspaper recently proclaimed: 'People who worry about what they look like when they are eating are the type of people who worry about what they look like when they are having sex.'

My response to this is very simple: eat like a pig and you won't make it to the 'Fancy coming in for a coffee?' stage, never mind make it to the bedroom. It is, of course, true that some things can be eaten in a very messy and seductive way, in which case you probably won't make it to pudding!

Eating is as fundamental to us as breathing. It is very important, however, to learn good manners, as they help to smooth our way in the company of others. A society devoid of manners would be a jagged and jarring society of clumsiness and unfriendly behaviour, a world without 'please' and 'thank you'.

The way we eat gives away a great deal about us: this very public exhibition is impossible to hide and says more about us in one mouthful than our entire CV. One *faux pas* too far and all could be lost and, believe me, it's amazing what a knife and fork will betray!

In the same way as there are set and understood rules for driving a car and behaving on the highway, so there are rules governing the way we should eat – a sort of 'dining way code' if you like.

Table manners have been passed down from generation to generation for hundreds of years, and throughout history, eating together has been an important and pleasant social event. The words 'company' and 'companion' come from the Latin *com* meaning 'with' and the Latin *panis* meaning 'bread' (see, I was concentrating in those Latin lessons!). A companion is therefore someone we eat with.

Table manners are older than tables themselves. Some 9,000 years ago people would cook soups in large pots and then dip their bone or wooden spoons into the pot to eat. The higher up the social scale you were determined when you had your turn at dipping. Some Arctic Inuit families still cook and eat from a common pot, with the men dipping first, then the women and then the children, sometimes with their fingers.

When the Roman Empire fell in AD 476, with it went the practice of lying down to eat, propped up on one arm and eating with the fingers of the free hand. Eating with the fingers has never fully disappeared. In Northern India, some diners use only the fingertips of the right hand, while in the South of the continent they use both hands. In fact, worldwide, more people eat with their fingers or chopsticks than use knives and forks but all cultures have rules about eating politely.

During the Crusades, knights learned not to lick their fingers but instead to wipe them on the tablecloth, and also not to smack their lips or snort while eating. They learned court-esy – how to behave at court.

Around 1669, King Louis XIV of France became the first person in Europe to offer his guests a place setting with knives, forks and spoons; he ordered that the knives should have rounded ends to prevent injury should things turn ugly.

Nowadays, if you exhibit bad table manners you might just as well have a flashing sign around your neck that says, 'Look at me, I am drawing attention to myself; I don't know how to behave, and I am socially inept.' Better, surely, to give out a signal that says, 'I am confident, I know what to do.' Those with the flashing signs are seldom invited back. And one thing is for sure, no one will correct you (actually, it is bad manners to do so) but they will certainly judge you!

There is nothing more off-putting than sitting at the same dining table with someone with appalling table manners – you know the sort of thing: eating with the mouth open (doing an impression of a cement mixer); making dog-like slurping noises; talking and gesticulating while eating; gulping at drinks and burping; constantly scraping knife over fork to remove an abnormal amount of food build-up; resting elbows on the table with knife and fork stuck up like oars; holding the knife poised as if ready to sign a cheque; elbows stuck so far out as to resemble a black London taxi with both doors open; hunching over the plate, guarding it from some unseen predator, and shovelling in huge mouthfuls as if the food is just about to be taken away. Not a pretty picture, is it?

This guide is designed to help ensure you're not one of these dreaded dining companions; it's not an attack or a criticism or, for that matter, a disguised patronising swipe at the uninitiated. If you follow the ways set out and illustrated in this book, you will be able to sit at any dining table with total confidence, safe in the knowledge that you know what to do.

HAND TO MOUTH

Hey, diddle diddle,
The cat and the fiddle,
The cow jumped over the moon,
The little dog laughed to see such sport,
And the dish ran away with the spoon.

Learning table manners starts from an early age. A small
spoon is one of the first objects baby zooms in on, mainly
because it is carrying dinner. Most new parents slip
liquefied nourishment into baby with a small spoon,
usually plastic in some jolly colour or another, and
sometimes featuring on the handle a recognisable cartoon
character, obviously meaningful only to the parents and
of no interest whatsoever to the liquefied-food recipient.

Traditionally, it was only the offspring of the seriously
wealthy that were fed from silverware – hence the
expression 'born with a silver spoon in the mouth'.

As the child progresses, spoon training starts in earnest
and it isn't long before the little one tries to wrest the
spoon from the feeder, maybe to load dinner faster (or it
could, of course, be a territorial thing; however, it's not
really for me to speculate, and such theories are perhaps
a little too deep for these pages – I am, after all, no

Benjamin Spock). Anyway, training starts and Junior is encouraged to hold a spoon and pusher: this combination of utensils is still available to this day in department and mother-and-baby stores, and is often given to baby as a christening present. These tools are sometimes fashioned from sterling silver but more often than not are made of 18/8 stainless steel (see page 126). The spoon is the well-known traditional shape, while the pusher is shaped like a miniature garden rake with a solid pushing face replacing the divided 'teeth' – ideal for pushing cut-up solids onto the spoon. With guidance, both of these training tools can be held neatly and correctly by even the tiniest of hands, and it is right here that the ground rules can begin to be burnt onto the 'table manners' CD.

After a while, set number two – known as a Progress Set – is introduced, which consists of a half adult-sized knife, fork and spoon, also available at good department stores.

WINING AND DINING

TAKE A SEAT

When arriving at a restaurant table, it is considered polite
for the gents to offer ladies seats facing into the restaurant
so that they get a more interesting view; I would try to
avoid my guests facing a back wall – it's always worth
booking ahead to guarantee a good table. A little forward
planning never goes amiss.

At a larger affair, the table may have been organised so
that the men and ladies sit alternately, but not necessarily
husband next to wife or partner next to partner. This is a
way of mixing people up and getting strangers to meet.
It is the done thing to speak to the guests seated on each
side of you and it's perfectly fine to speak to the guests
opposite. Where once sex, religion and politics were
taboo subjects for table conversation, these days pretty
much anything goes; however, medical procedures, illness
and money are still beyond the pale and should be
avoided. Showing off about a recent trip around the
world can be very irritating to people, as can great
detailed monologues about your latest automotive
acquisition – this and similar 'boasts' may be considered
gauche, anyway, so best avoided as well.

When places are found, the gentleman should always
'seat' the lady on his right by pulling out her chair and

helping her closer to the table before sitting down himself, but never before the hostess is seated. Where there is a butler present, he will pull the chairs out for the ladies. Sorry, guys, old-fashioned it might be, but no removing jackets while at the table, at least not if it is a formal affair. In some of the finest hotels and restaurants in the land there is still a dining dress code, usually jacket and tie.

It's probably best not to get up and leave the table before the host or hostess does so, and minors should definitely wait until their elders have decided to leave the table, although they can, of course, ask permission to leave. The question is always: 'May I get down, please?'

Don't be surprised to find an extra place set at the table for an imaginary person if you are one of thirteen guests; tradition and superstition demands the extra place setting. When everyone is seated, the extra visitor's place is cleared. This rather bizarre tradition can be traced as far back as Norse mythology, and, as we all know, there were thirteen people present at the Last Supper, Judas Iscariot being the thirteenth. Napoleon of France would summon a professional 'fourteenth' diner to avoid the possibility of bad luck. This ritual is very much a part of

European table etiquette today and is still practised by the Ritz Hotel in London. At the Savoy Hotel, a wooden cat named 'Caspar' is placed as the fourteenth guest and even has meals served to him.

plate expectations

Never be rude or patronising to the people serving you – it's never justified, whether they are young, inexperienced school leavers or ex-public school university graduates. If you do have a complaint about the staff, either leave or tell the management, but it is highly recommended that if you stay, you complain after you have eaten. There is no reason why you should pay for cold or sub-standard food. If you intend to complain about the food, be sure to do so politely and assertively because, in my experience, restaurant staff can be very imaginative when it comes to getting their own back! If everyone agrees that the offering is inedible, just refuse to pay.

Once seated, you can expect to be served at table from the left and have your empty plates removed from the left; your drinks, wines, water and coffee will be served from the right.

If you are served by a butler you can expect to have your plate given to you from the left and removed from the right; your wines, etc. will be served from the right. There are variations to these rules, of course, and these you need not be too worried about as none of them can be said to be wrong.

Some butlers will serve all liquids from the right, including soup, while others will serve plates from the left, soup from the left and also clear from the left. It is worth keeping an eye on what is going on around you; your plates will always arrive from the left and your drinks from the right, but your empty plates could be removed from either side. If in doubt, just sit back slightly and wait because you can be sure your place will be cleared!

Acknowledge your waiter by all means, but thanking him every time he refills your glass is annoying; the first time he says in answer to your thanks, 'Don't mention it', take it that he means it. Speaking to the waiter in his native tongue if you are not absolutely fluent is absurd and will make your guests cringe; the waiter is bound to humiliate you by answering in English anyway. If you have problems pronouncing a long complicated name, just shorten it or point at the menu, the waiter will know what you mean. If you do not know the answer to the question, 'How would you like it cooked?', don't be afraid to let the chef decide, and if you are worried that there is a chance your steak may be overcooked, order it rare – you can always send it back for another go in the pan if it arrives too bloody. An overcooked piece of meat is a complete and unforgivable waste.

Hotel and restaurant service is based on Silver Service. You won't get the whole meal plated, like in a high street breakfast cafe; what you will receive is the item you ordered from the menu already plated and brought to your place – this is, after all, the platform for the chef's art, his *raison d'être*. Vegetables and sauces will be brought to the table separately for you to serve yourself. Simply use a serving spoon and fork to take a small amount and don't forget there are others at the table still to serve themselves.

As the meal progresses, you may feel the need to go to the loo – nothing wrong with this, of course, although try not to disappear halfway through a course; despite the fact that it's a bit unsavoury, it can be a real conversation-breaker and appear a little rude.

At a large function like a wedding reception you can expect real Silver Service. You will be given an empty plate and the waiter or waitress will serve you from the left. He or she will hold a large serving dish with one hand and serve you by grasping your allowance in between a serving spoon and fork held in the other hand, and will place this portion on your plate. Spoons and forks held in this manner are referred to as a clamp.

Vegetables and sauces will either be placed on the table for you to serve yourself or in some cases be brought to the table by another waiter who will serve you. It is far better just to let it happen, but if you are given something that you really don't like, don't make a fuss; it is perfectly acceptable to leave it.

Butler service is quite different. You will be given a plate, the butler will then leave the dining room and return with a serving dish, which is more often than not a silver serving plate containing the meat or fish course, and offer it to you from your left. Simply pick up the serving spoon in one hand and the serving fork in the other – they will be facing you on the serving dish – and serve yourself; there is no need to rush, the butler will hold the serving plate just above the table perfectly still and fairly close to your plate for as long as you take. As a point of interest, the butler will never let the plate touch the table, it just isn't done, so don't press down too hard on the serving dish. If the butler is working alone, as soon as he has offered the first serving plate to everyone he will leave the dining room and return with another plate of vegetables and you simply serve yourself as before. Sauces and mustards will arrive last; sauces may also be offered to you by the butler: just use the ladle in the sauceboat and take some, replacing the ladle when you have enough. There is no need to take a huge amount of anything as the butler will return to offer you more.

If the party is a large one, there may be two butlers and other serving staff; all this really means is that you will be served slightly more quickly but the process is the same.

Throughout the butler-served meal your water glass will be refilled and possibly your wine glass as well, but often the host prefers to serve wines to his guests. Don't be tempted to lift your glass to get a refill in an attempt to help the butler or waiter; actually it is more of a nuisance as a moving target is quite difficult to hit at times. It is perfectly acceptable for you to speak to the butler if you want something but please, please never ask for an ashtray!

The essential difference with butler service is that you take what you want; it is not for the butler to give you what he thinks you should have.

If you are attending an event that has a buffet, you will be expected to serve yourself. There really is only one rule: don't load your plate as if you are never going to eat again! It is definitely undignified and off-putting for other guests who will immediately notice any overt piggy behaviour! An overloaded plate at a buffet is not only difficult to negotiate with one hand but items are apt to drop off. At a very high-level sales meeting lunch about twenty years ago, I saw someone balance a side of smoked mackerel on the top of an already mountainous plate of food; the fish actually see-sawed over the mountain peak, eventually falling off the plate and landing squarely on the toe of one of the director's shoes – needless to say, a very embarrassing situation and one easily avoided. If you are very hungry, it is far better, if you must, to go to the buffet several times and take a small amount each time. In the case of a business lunch or buffet, even if alcohol is freely available, do not under any circumstances drink it.

napkin

napkin /nápkin/ *n* (in full table **napkin**) a square piece of linen, paper, etc. used for wiping the lips, fingers, etc. at meals, or serving fish, etc. on
English via Old French *nappe* tablecloth and from Latin *mappa*, sheet of cloth on which maps were once drawn

-kin a suffix meaning little, borrowed from Middle Dutch – *kijn* and Middle Low German – *kin* (modern German –chen). Fundamentally, *nap*, *nape*, cloth and –*kin*, thus little cloth

Source, *Oxford English Dictionary,* Ninth edition and *Chambers Dictionary of Etymology,* 2004 edition

The main function of this small square of starched linen at the table is to protect your clothing from spillages and dropped pieces of food during dinner – I'm sure all of us at one time or another have ended up with food in our laps.

It's rather different these days but you can imagine how useful this device was at the medieval table, when diners needed a large sheet tied behind their necks and draped over their bellies in an effort to protect them from the enthusiastic meat-tearing and gorging, and to wipe their hands clean of peacock and swan fat.

The napkin is a spin-off of our baby bib days and is just as essential now as it was then. I have had the misfortune to sit with people who could have done with one of those bibs with a trough. (I think it's called a 'pelican' bib, for fairly obvious reasons.)

The other use of the napkin is to keep the area around our mouths clean and crumb-free and, of course, to wipe our hands on as some foods are still eaten with the fingers.

Your napkin will be placed within your 'dining area', that is to say no further to the right than your first piece of cutlery and no further to the left than your bread plate. It is perfectly acceptable to find it placed on your bread plate or in the space that will later be occupied by your dinner plate. So you shouldn't really find yourself picking up your neighbour's by mistake.

Once seated, unfold your napkin and place it over your lap and, unless you are using it, keep it there until you have finished eating. Your napkin shouldn't really be tucked into your collar; however, some foods are potentially messy – shellfish, oysters and asparagus, for example – and in such cases I'm sure a napkin tucked into your collar wouldn't be frowned upon, providing it is positioned there as a temporary measure for the duration of that course. In some parts of Europe, in particular Switzerland, you may be offered a silver hook on which to hang your napkin.

To be very polite, one should never actually wipe around the mouth but simply dab at the corners of the mouth to remove crumbs; do this as a matter of course before drinking from a glass or cup and before leaving the table. You can, however, wipe your hands with your napkin.

If you need to get up and leave the table for any reason, leave your napkin on your seat; this is a signal to whoever is serving that you will be coming back and it avoids other diners from having to look at your soiled cloth.

If you drop your napkin during the proceedings, it is OK for you to pick it up. In fine dining establishments, or where there is a butler, you will be given a replacement if your napkin is seen on the floor; you are entitled, though, to ask for a clean napkin to replace the one you've picked up yourself – after all, who wants to have a 'dab' around the mouth with a piece of cloth covered with bits from the floor? (Remember, it is totally inappropriate to use the edge of the tablecloth!)

At the end of the meal and when everyone else has finished, you should gently refold your napkin (linen or paper) and place it to the left of your plate; never leave it crumpled and on the plate. You should also never do this with a paper napkin, the only possible exception being in the case of a finger buffet.

In some restaurants the waiters will bring you a sort of 'post dining' napkin – generally a small piece of towelling infused with a citrus flavour that comes hot from the microwave, ready for you to have a jolly good wipe and temporary wash with; in such situations it is perfectly OK to do so.

If your dinner menu includes something that is normally eaten with the fingers, you can expect to be given a 'finger bowl', which is usually a small bowl filled with warm water and some slices of lemon for you to dip your fingers in after eating to rinse them. Hands and fingers should then be dried on your napkin.

Napkins are usually folded and perfectly ironed when placed on the table, and come in a variety of shapes and sizes. One butler I knew was especially adept at rolling severely starched napkins like a tube with the family's crest perfectly centred and uppermost facing the diner, and at other times folded to resemble a large kipper tie with the point facing south. Napkins should be handled as little as possible; one very traditional style requires origami training and, after considerable folding, ends up looking like a hat worn by a *Thunderbirds* puppet: this is commonly known as a Bishop's Mitre and is capable of standing up unaided. (See pages 36 and 37 for how to fold a napkin into a Bishop's Mitre.)

You will find that in most cases the napkin will be simply folded and laid flat. If you are preparing napkins at home for dinner guests, just fold the linen squares into rectangles and iron flat. At breakfast or lunch, a triangle shape is fine, providing the long side runs parallel to the first piece of cutlery on the left with the middle point facing west.

Napkins are so commonly used that it would be impossible to finish a table setting without them. Napkins are there to be used, so make sure you do just that, unless you are happy to look like a spoon-fed baby with food on your cheeks!

SOME DON'TS FOR THE TABLE

DON'T lean back precariously onto the rear two legs of your chair.

*

DON'T throw an arm over the back of your chair.

*

DON'T stick a little finger out.

*

DON'T get up and leave before your host; minors should not leave before their elders without permission.

*

DON'T spit unwanted food into your napkin or your hand – remove it with your fork and place on the side of your plate. Olive stones and fish bones can be removed with your fingers.

This is how to make a napkin look like a Bishop's Mitre:

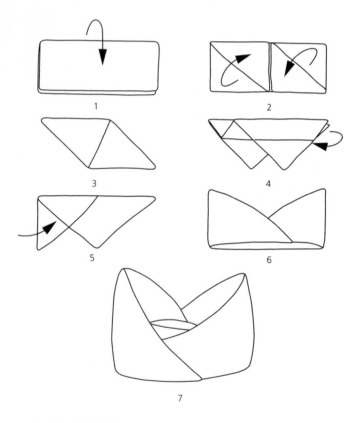

Illustration © 2006 Nicholas Clayton Enterprises.

Bishop's Mitre Napkin

1. Starting with a starched square napkin, fold in half.
2. Fold the corners to the centre.
3. Turn the napkin over and rotate by a quarter.
4. Fold the bottom edge up to the top edge and pull the point out from under the top fold.
5. Turn the left end into the pleat on the left to form a point on the left-hand side.
6. Turn the napkin over and turn the right-hand side end into the pleat, forming a point on the right-hand side.
7. Open the base and stand upright.

No one said it was easy.

you definitely need glasses

I have been known to drink white wine from virtually
any type of glass, cup or mug, which I suppose is a
disgrace in itself, but I'd sooner drink Champagne from
the bottle than drink it from a mug and, there is no
getting away from it, Guinness only tastes right from a
sleever* (see explanation below). All of this is to say that
the correct glass is vital.

Different wine regions in Europe have, over the years,
developed traditional glasses considered ideal for
drinking specific wine types. A wine glass should be held
by its stem, which prevents the hand warming a cool
wine. The glass is tulip- or onion-shaped and curves
inwards to retain the bouquet and to allow the wine to
be swirled around gently to release the aroma. A white
wine glass is smaller and shorter than one for red wine
but almost always the same shape. A water glass doesn't
usually have a stem. Champagne is served these days in a
long, thin, stemmed glass called a flute, designed to
contain the bubbles for longer.

*To most people in the UK, a straight-sided pint beer glass is a
'straight' but in Bristol it is known as a 'sleever'.

different types of drinking glasses

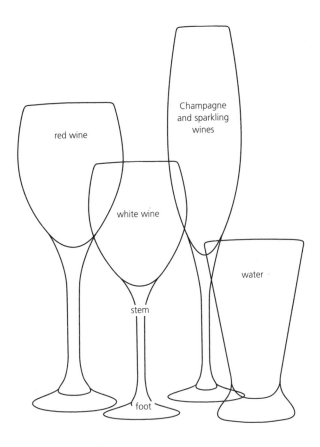

red wine

Champagne and sparkling wines

white wine

water

stem

foot

arrangement of drinking glasses
(guide only as positions may vary)

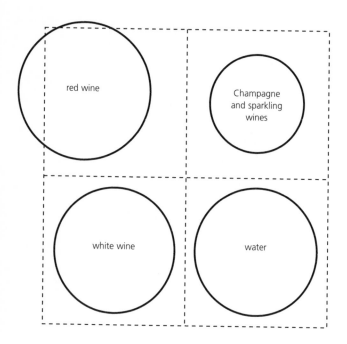

When setting the dining table, the drinking glasses are arranged in a certain pattern, with the taller glasses furthest away, so that you can pick up the shorter glasses at the front without having to reach awkwardly over the high ones.

Broadly speaking, if you imagine a square divided into four sections, it's a safe bet to assume that you will find your red wine glass in the top left-hand square, your white wine glass in the bottom left-hand square and the water glass in the bottom right-hand square. The water glass will probably be placed in line with the top of the main course knife. The top right-hand space is reserved for non-standard glasses that may be set in place towards the end of your meal or for earlier or later courses, for example Champagne flutes or smaller glasses for dessert wine or port. If you set a table with fewer glasses than the four shown (e.g. a red wine and a water glass only), still place them in the correct imaginary square.

Your water glass may be filled, and refilled, to about three-quarters. Red and white wine is poured, and refilled, to about half a glass. You should never be given or serve a full glass of wine!

Don't be insulted if you are handed a third of a glass of Champagne, this is perfect etiquette: hold a full glass of Champagne for half an hour and it becomes too warm to drink and quite unpalatable.

Drinking glasses should sparkle without a fingermark or smudge in sight; if yours are dirty, send them back. In my view the same can be said for the other type of glasses, because it is, after all, hard to be optimistic with a misty optic.

drink

In hotel dining rooms and restaurants it is customary to be given the opportunity to try the wine you have chosen before accepting it. In polite society this would always be considered the man's prerogative. The wine waiter will almost certainly pour a small amount of wine into the man's glass for him to taste, the idea being that the wine should be deemed decent before serving it to a lady. I don't see why the ladies shouldn't have a taste as well – after all, he might like it and she may not. But it's tradition. Generally, the person paying the bill always tastes the wine; if a man is being wined and dined by a woman, then it is she who performs the tasting, no matter how much the waiter may insist otherwise.

If you feel slightly dazed by the wine list, ask the sommelier (*som-el-ee-ay*) for advice. It's his job to select the wines and he probably knows better than you what you will enjoy. It's amazing, too, how some sommeliers have a knack of knowing how much you are willing to spend and make suggestions accordingly.

Once the wine is poured, pick up the glass by the stem and give the wine a quick sniff; if it seems pleasant, drink a small amount and let it flush around your mouth before swallowing it to really get to grips with the flavours; don't be afraid to do this a couple of times because the true identity often only surfaces the second time.

If you really don't like the wine and your dining partner agrees, then this is the time to say so. Perfect etiquette on the part of the wine waiter demands an immediate replacement after you have been given the chance for another flick through the wine list. There should be no tut-tutting, rolling of eyes or funny looks from the waiter – wine has to be right and you are paying.

Don't expect to get an exchange if you accept the bottle then drink half, or find it clashes with the starter; it just won't happen unless, of course, you are willing to pay for it. A dining partner and I experienced refusal in a very snooty little hotel in North Dorset where our protestations about a really lousy wine were met with a sensational level of frosty rudeness; granted the wine list was poor, making choice difficult, but it was served too warm and tasted awful. What's more, my vastly over-priced pre-dinner bottle of lager was room temperature, and why do the bar staff in these places always put all the tonic in a vodka and tonic without asking? We haven't been back, obviously. If you expect good food, then good service and well-kept wines should be of equal quality.

A corked wine is not difficult to spot – it is not a wine with pieces of cork floating in caused by bad corkscrew action, but one which is fatally flawed through infection. Real cork is cut from the bark of the Cork Oak (*Quercus suber*) grown in countries that are a lot hotter than the British Isles. By its very nature, therefore, there is a possibility that infection may creep in. The mouldy, musty old socks and wet cardboard and even rotting mushrooms aroma is caused by *Trichloranisol*, one of a group of compounds that is activated during the cork cleaning process. Once smelled, never forgotten. Fortunately, it doesn't happen very often and no decent sommelier or wine waiter would disagree with this complaint. Wines can taste vinegary sometimes, so if you don't like the aroma send it back. If the white wine you ordered appears too deep a colour it may be oxidised (spoiled by contact with the air) – it will smell and taste dull and stale; poor storage or faulty corks can spoil wine in the best cellars.

These days it is considered very ill-mannered to get drunk. If it happens to you, best to just make yourself scarce and preferably in a taxi.

and some more hints...

- There are no rules about eating the garnish that decorates your dinner but I think most people would leave it, no matter how appetising the scene from *Swan Lake* looks whittled from a carrot. Feel free, however, to eat whatever comes with your cocktail (not the umbrella or the sparkler, obviously).

after dinner

There might be a toast or two raised. If you are asked to stand up for a toast, do so but do not 'chink' glasses, as it is just not done.

Do not smoke before, during or after dinner at the table! And please don't ask for an ashtray. If you must smoke, go somewhere else – the car park is good!

Speeches can be eye-wateringly dreadful and embarrassing. Sometimes they are terrific, of course, but at other times you wish you were somewhere else altogether. It is, however, extremely bad manners to start a conversation with the person next to you during a speech. If the speech contains jokes or attempts at jokes it's good manners to laugh a little. The idea is to help the speechmaker feel at ease and that he or she is doing OK. Booing, heckling and throwing things are definitely out of the question.

Port is traditionally served after dinner; it is a fortified wine, which means it contains brandy. Its colour can be as red as red wine or almost clear. Port is drunk from a small glass, probably with a stem and shaped like a wine glass.

Old British naval tradition has it that the host will pour a glass of port for the guest on his right, then pass the bottle or decanter to the left, with each person filling his or her glass then passing on to the next person on the left; the bottle should never touch down onto the table until it arrives back with the host, who pours himself a glass of port.

leaving

Very formal invitations might state 'Carriages at Midnight', for example, which is a very old-fashioned way of letting you know when the proceedings will finish. This is actually very useful if you need to order a cab in advance.

It is very good manners to thank the host when you leave but keep it short and simple. If you really enjoyed yourself, follow up with a thank you note. If you were not so enamoured with the evening, do not write to your host to say so because this faux pas is one faux pas too far.

SOME DON'TS FOR THE TABLE

DON'T eat chicken legs or chops with your fingers (you can do what you like at home).

*

DON'T use plastic, spiky handles to hold corn on the cob – they really are too silly; use both hands.

*

DON'T talk with your mouth full, and eat small amounts at a time so that, if necessary, you can keep a conversation going.

*

DON'T overload your fork and shove huge amounts into your mouth in one go.

*

DON'T eat as if you have only moments to live; always eat slowly.

DON'T add any more food if your mouth is full.

*

DON'T eat with your elbows stuck out like wings; keep them by your sides.

*

DON'T point with your cutlery.

*

DON'T hold onto your fork while drinking.

*

DON'T use your napkin while holding your knife.

*

DON'T polish the cutlery with your napkin; if the utensils look grubby, ask for replacements.

*

DON'T pick up dropped cutlery; ask for replacements.

AT THE TABLE

THE BASIC RULES

cutlery

In Britain there are very specific rules about using cutlery. In the US and Europe, many people have a rather different way of wielding their eating implements.

Generally speaking, these diners in foreign lands hold their knife and fork like the British – that is to say, knife in one hand, fork in the other – only until they have finished cutting their food. They hold the fork like a dagger to stab meat so as not to let it escape from the plate during cutting. Once the meat is cut up, they put their knife down on the side of the plate, transfer the fork to the right hand and, with the tines (prongs) facing up, scoop up the cut food. By which time the elbow of the left arm is resting on the table. In spite of this, the British holding method is known as Continental and the American method is, well, American. Both are perfectly acceptable etiquette.

The British, on the other hand, hold the knife in the right hand and the fork in the left for the duration of the meal; the soup and pudding spoons are held in the right hand

and pudding fork in the left. Interestingly, some left-handed people do the same while others do the whole thing the other way round. My mother is a perfect example of this – although she is a true left-hander, she uses cutlery like a right-hander.

If you have a look in the cutlery section of any large department store, you will find handfuls of shiny equipment, all with specific jobs – carving, serving, eating – you name it.

Depending on menu choice, the cutlery will differ. I doubt if you will ever sit down faced with more than three items per hand but it can sometimes happen. However, for demonstration purposes, my table is restricted to one set of knives, forks and spoons.

The following illustrated section is designed to help you understand how to hold cutlery and in which order to pick up the various pieces of the basic kit, with a few illustrations showing how **not** to hold cutlery.

a place setting for three courses

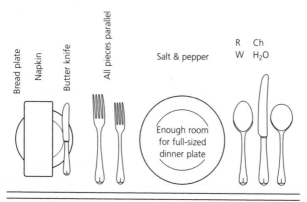

Bread plate
Napkin
Butter knife
All pieces parallel
Salt & pepper
R   Ch
W H_2O

Enough room for full-sized dinner plate

Middle of bread plate in line with centre of dinner plate

Table edge

All pieces in line and parallel to table edge

R – red wine   Ch – Champagne
W – white wine H_2O – water

the setting

Opposite is an illustration of cutlery set for three courses – soup, main course and pudding. Pudding is always pudding, by the way, not dessert, which is a separate course after pudding. The use of the word dessert is derived from the French *desservir* – to clear away – so it is served when all other courses have been cleared and usually consists of fruit.

All cutlery items for all courses are always placed parallel to each other, facing north to south. The tines of forks should be placed facing up and the cutting edges of knives are always placed facing **west**, never east! The bases of the handles should all be in line and parallel to the table edge; a simple way to check this is to use a thumb (see illustration on page 133). Enough room should be allowed between the cutlery for a full-sized dinner plate – the cutlery should not be obscured when the plate is set down. (When dining, never touch or move your plate once it has been placed in front of you.)

In addition to the cutlery, the table would also be set with a bread plate, knife and napkin for each diner. The bread plate is always placed on the left-hand side of each setting – if you remember this, you'll never eat your neighbour's bread! The butter knife is used to butter pieces of bread that you have broken with your fingers (see page 58). Glasses for white and red wine and water would also be positioned near each place setting.

Salt and pepper should also be on the table; if you want to use either and can't reach them, ask for them to be passed to you. Do not get out of your seat or reach across the table. If you are asked for the salt or the pepper individually, pass both because they should always go together.

go!

The rule is not to start eating until everyone has been served. If there are only two of you, or a small group, this rule still holds. When a larger group gathers together, it is often logistically impossible for the kitchen to get all the plates out together, so to avoid eating cold food, it is permissible to start before others have received their food. A quick nod to the host with a 'May I?' is deemed polite.

When dining, start with the cutlery on the outside left and right of the place setting and work inwards for each

quick guide to using cutlery

Work inwards from the outside using the next piece of cutlery.

subsequent course. If the starter is soup, the spoon will not have a corresponding item of cutlery.

bread

Never cut bread or bread rolls. Break the bread with your fingers and butter a small piece at a time with the knife that you will find either on the bread plate on the left of your last piece of cutlery on this side, or just to the right of it on the table.

The only time it is permissible to butter a piece of bread without breaking it is at breakfast when a slice of toast has probably been cut in half already.

the late mr and mrs

An important note on etiquette: If you find you can no longer make it to the dinner party or other occasion, do let the organisers or hosts know as early as possible. The same applies if you are going to be late; to turn up late without prior warning to your hosts is just plain rude and disrespectful to them and the other guests.

and some more hints…

- It's up to you how much salt you put on your food but be careful not to insult your host by adding salt before you have tasted your food.

- Each time you take a mouthful, lean over the plate; if anything falls, it will land on the plate and not in your lap.

- If you are holding a plate, never take a piece of crudité or a canapé and put it straight into your mouth; it should touch down on your plate first.

- Never put used cutlery back down onto the table.

first course — soup

Hold the soup spoon as shown below; this is one of the
three times that such a grip is permitted, the others being
for holding a fish knife and a pudding spoon.

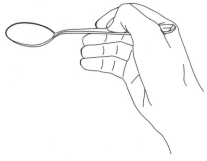

Passing your spoon across the soup in a south to north
direction (see below), gently dip the spoon in and pick up
some soup.

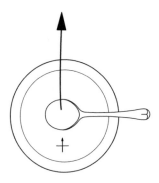

Holding the spoon to your mouth (see below), quietly 'drink' from the spoon.

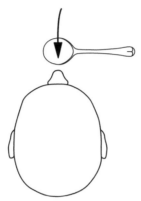

When there is only a small amount left in the bowl, lift it from the edge closest to you, tilting it away from you, and spoon up the remaining soup, as shown below.

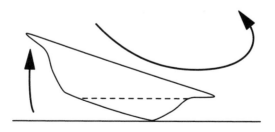

When you have finished, leave the bowl with the spoon as shown in the 'finished' position below. The illustration also shows the position in which the spoon should be placed when 'resting' between mouthfuls.

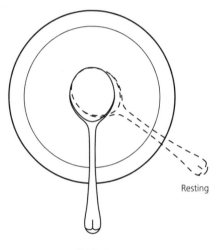

Resting

Finished

main course

Hold the knife and fork as illustrated below – no other grip is allowed!

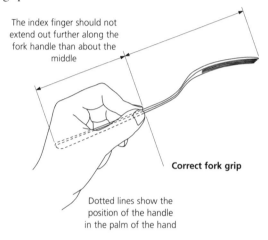

The index finger should not extend out further along the fork handle than about the middle

Correct fork grip

Dotted lines show the position of the handle in the palm of the hand

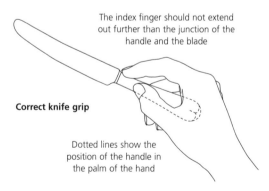

The index finger should not extend out further than the junction of the handle and the blade

Correct knife grip

Dotted lines show the position of the handle in the palm of the hand

Keep the fork tines facing down at all times. **Only** your fork goes in your mouth; your knife is used to cut and as a pusher but **never** enters your mouth.

The handles of both the knife and the fork should rest comfortably in the palm of each hand, with an index finger extended along the top of the knife and the fork handle to exert pressure.

Keep the fork tines down and load food onto the fork by pushing against the knife; with practice, even the awkward green pea can be transported en masse like this.

Never lift anything with the fork tines up, or change cutlery from one hand to the other.

pudding

If you are given a pudding fork, always use it as it avoids chasing your food around the plate to get it on the spoon (using a finger as a pusher is not acceptable in the adult world). Hold the fork tines down and grip it as you would a main course fork but **never** actually put it in your mouth.

The spoon is held like a main course knife (see below), as some cutting or dividing might be needed; in such cases, use the left edge of the spoon bowl as you would a knife.

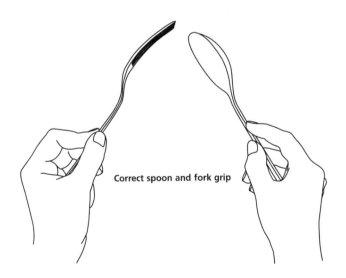

Correct spoon and fork grip

As the spoon is lifted to the mouth, and the wrist revolves, the handle grip changes to the soup grip (as seen below).

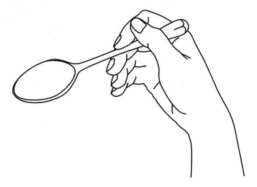

The pudding spoon angle of approach to the mouth is different from the one used for soup (see below).

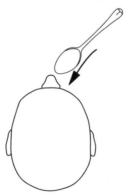

The illustrations below show the correct positions for your pudding fork and spoon when 'resting' between mouthfuls and when you have finished eating.

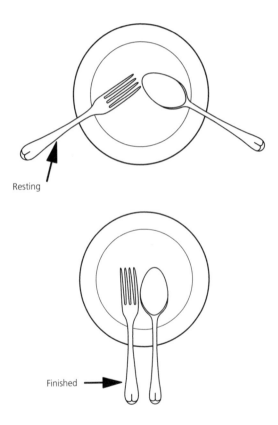

Resting

Finished

the alternative pudding spoon and fork location

You will probably see pudding spoons and forks set like this on many occasions and there is nothing wrong with it, although you probably won't see it in top restaurants, hotels or tables set by a modern butler.

It dates back from the days when a meal consisted of a huge number of courses and there possibly wasn't enough space for all the cutlery alongside the place setting; in such instances, the butler would 'draw down' the spoon and fork after all the other cutlery had been cleared.

and some more hints...

- De-juice a lemon wedge by holding it over your dinner and twisting the prongs of your fork into the flesh.

- Split the bill by all means, but if you are obviously the biggest earner then you should pay more or at least offer to do so.

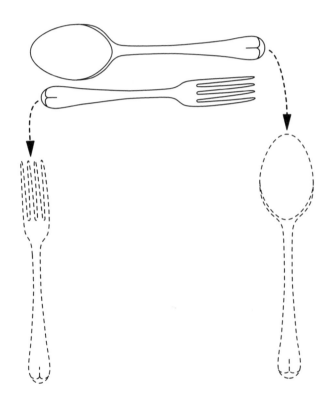

'I'm coming back/resting' and 'I've finished.'

If you stop eating for a short period of time, it could look as if you have given up or you have finished. To guard against having your plate removed before you have finished eating, you should always leave your cutlery as shown opposite top. Your cutlery should be placed on your plate and never 'gang-planked' at an angle from the table to the plate. Do not leave half-eaten food on the fork when you put it down.

When you have finished eating, leave your cutlery on the plate as shown opposite bottom. These signals should be recognised by the waiters.

and some more hints...

- Eat quietly; the essence of good table manners is unobtrusiveness.

- Take one canapé at a time, not a handful; it is the waiter's job to make sure you are offered more.

'I'm coming back/resting'

Never leave food on your fork
when you put it down

'I've finished'

main
course

soup

pudding

DON'T EVEN THINK ABOUT IT

The following illustrations show how **not** to hold cutlery, although the one below is actually the correct way to hold a fish knife, an item of cutlery seldom seen these days.

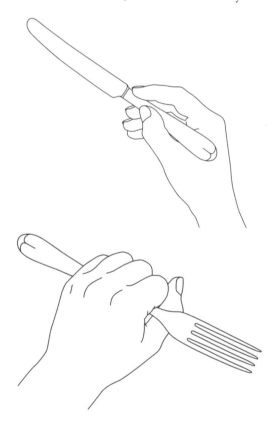

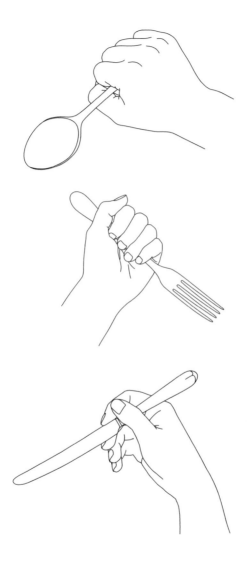

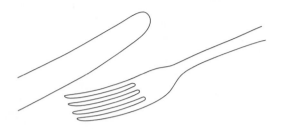

Do **not** do anything with the fork tines facing up or put your knife in your left hand (unless, of course, you are left-handed).

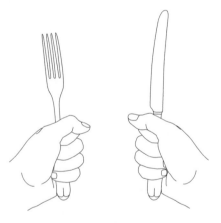

Do not sit and wait for your food with your knife and fork held like this. Do not hold your knife and fork in these positions when chewing a mouthful of food. In short, **never** do this (don't laugh, I've seen it dozens of times!).

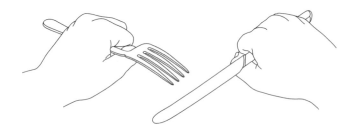

Your knife and fork should never be raised more than
2 or 3 inches (5–8 cm) above your plate; remember this
rule and you will never cut your tongue!

Don't clean off excess built-up food from either your
knife or fork by scraping one over the other up in the air;
if you must do this, do so slowly and quietly with your
cutlery down on your plate.

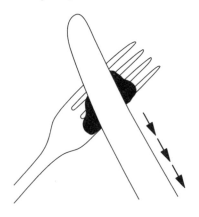

BITING TALK

I follow an obsessional oral hygiene regime born partly out of the obvious necessity to nurture the products of hefty investment, and partly because of my own dental background.

During my years at the Royal Dental Hospital in London in the 1970s, I saw some amazing horrors caused by neglect. Having witnessed this devastation, I sure as hell am determined the same won't happen to me.

The point is that a clean up after eating is no bad thing. Humans have been scraping around their teeth forever. Skulls of Neanderthals and homo sapiens have shown clear signs that their teeth had been poked at with some type of early toothpick. Virtually no one goes out to eat with a toothbrush in their pocket (well, OK, I do, but that's different).

Restaurants have supplied toothpicks for years and there are rules of etiquette for their use.

- Before gouging around with a pick, try a swill of water to free the problem.

- Go somewhere to probe the teeth in private, never do it at the table.

- Never do that thing with a flattened hand over the top lip in a failed attempt to hide the picking going on underneath; this is unparalleled in its vulgarity and, in my view, on a par with sniffing.

- Don't use your fingers to pick your teeth.

- Never use your knife or your fork for tooth-picking; if this practice were any more taboo, it would be illegal.

- Don't polish your front teeth with your napkin.

- If you are really stuck, a matchstick can be used, but not at the table.

- It's probably best for artificial teeth-wearers to slip away to give them a hose off in private. I know it might sound obvious, but I have actually seen some taken out for checking at the table!

- Be aware, no one likes to see teeth decorated with spinach.

SOME DON'TS FOR THE TABLE

DON'T forget to pay the bill/tip.

*

DON'T treat the waiting staff badly, or you might end up with more than you ordered.

*

DON'T say, 'my man' as in 'Bring me some Champagne, my man' to a butler or a waiter – it's insulting.

*

DON'T gulp at drinks; it looks desperate and greedy.

*

DON'T make a fuss: if you don't like something, just leave it.

*

DON'T take the rest of your pint to the table. Finish it or leave it.

DON'T pick your teeth (or anything else, for that matter!) at the table.

*

DON'T lift your glass for a refill, as a moving target can be difficult to hit.

*

DON'T blow on hot food or drink to cool it; just wait until it has reached a comfortable temperature.

*

DON'T smoke anything at the table...........ever!

*

DON'T get drunk; you'll look absurd.

*

DON'T photograph the buffet.

*

DON'T move your plate after you have been served; it just isn't done.

FOOD FOR THOUGHT

SOME DIFFICULT FOODS

artichoke

The globe artichoke is a sauce- or butter-dipping
exercise. Part of the thistle family, the artichoke has been
cultivated for centuries and is one of the oldest foods
eaten by humans. Grown extensively in France, artichoke
production also became very popular in America and has
an interesting history there; Marilyn Monroe, for
example, became the first Artichoke Queen in California
in 1947.

Using your fingers, break off the leaves one at a time
and, holding the point, dip the wide end into the butter
or sauce and suck out the fleshy insides by drawing the
leaf through your teeth. Then place the fibrous remains
onto your plate. Just before you get to the centre, the
leaves will become pale and purplish in colour with a
sort of fuzzy middle; this you can discard, leaving the
heart. Using a knife and fork, slice and eat this as you
would a fillet steak. I first ordered a globe artichoke in
the Café de Paris in Monte Carlo about twenty-five years
ago and ended up covered in *hollandaise* sauce, after
which I needed a good wipe around. This cleaning up
exercise was well timed as, half an hour later, I met and

shook hands with the now late David Niven, who had been lunching in the Hotel de Paris.

asparagus

Asparagus, a member of the lily family and cultivated for 2,000 years, could be a potential problem to the uninitiated. Traditionally, these wonderful boiled green stems are served as a starter with melted butter to dip them in.

Using your left hand, pick up one stem at a time by the thickest end and dip the 'spear' end into the liquid butter; bite off a short piece at a time – don't shove the whole thing in, in one go. The slightly woody end that you held may be discarded. If the stems are very long, it is permitted to cut them shorter and carry on with the fingers. There is a thicker white variety grown in Europe, sometimes between the rows of hops in Bavaria, and these you will find on menus for a short season only as a main course – they are eaten with a knife and fork. The flavour of this white asparagus is a bit flat compared with the green variety grown in the British Isles. Another thing worth mentioning is the strange aroma when you pass water after eating asparagus – it is very strong and unmistakeable but nothing to worry about. (I've been told that it shows good kidney function.)

cheese

In common with the French we, too, have some rules about eating cheese. It is not so much the eating that matters, but more the way it is cut. Round varieties like Camembert should be sliced from the centre and cut like pieces of a pie, into small wedges. Pieces of cheese that are much larger but already resemble a wedge should be cut from the 'nose' – that is to say the sharp end – first.

chinese, japanese and indian food

Most people I know tend to eat curry using a fork in their right hand and a piece of dahl-roti in the other as a sort of scoop or a pusher. It is also OK to use a spoon and fork and this is often a preferred option. Only if you are invited to a very authentic Asian dinner will you be expected to eat with your fingers, as it is the traditional and correct way to eat. With the back of your hand facing uppermost and your fingers fully extended downwards, bring all fingertips and thumb together to very gently pick up a small amount of food at a time; lean over your plate when eating from your fingers.

I just cannot get on with chopsticks and have never been refused a knife and fork in a Chinese restaurant. If you are invited to a dinner where everyone is using chopsticks, it might be an idea to follow suit, and, of course, eating sushi demands an attempt at least to use chopsticks. If you want to persevere, this is one way to do it.........Good luck.

1 Take one stick and lay it across your hand so that it rests in the space between your index finger and thumb; if you are right-handed, your right hand.
2 Let the end of the stick rest on the inside of your middle finger. This stick does not move.
3 Now take the second stick and lay it on top of the first.
4 Grasp the second stick between thumb and index finger. You can now move the stick up and down using it to trap food against the stationary stick.

It's easy with practice.........allegedly.

Just out of interest, people from Southeast Asia use a spoon and fork and keep their chopsticks for their noodle course.

corn-on-the-cob

You probably won't come across corn-on-the-cob at a formal function. It is very difficult to eat without getting into a mess, and it is notorious for getting stuck in your teeth. If you are faced with it at an informal gathering, the politest way to eat it is to use your fingers. Using both hands, hold the cob at the very ends (avoid using those silly little plastic corn-on-the-cob look-alike forkettes).

escargots

As a fanatical gardener, I spend an inordinate amount of time trying to trap these things and rid my beds of them. I know the edible ones are a different variety but I still find the whole thing disagreeable – I think it's the thought of the trails that they leave.

If you must eat snails, just hold the shell with the rounded clamp that you are given, and turn the snail meat out with the special fork that is also provided and pop the whole creature in, in one go. They are often served in a garlic butter sauce, so it is an idea to have your napkin to hand. It's perfectly in order to give these a good chew and, if my experience is anything to go by, secure teeth are vital!

fish

I would guess that most of the fish eaten in the British Isles is filleted before it reaches the table, as is nearly all of the fish bought from the chip shop. Fish bones are notoriously dangerous. Inadvertently swallowed, they can become lodged in the throat leaving the only chance of removal the accident and emergency department of the local hospital. If you are served a piece of fish that has been filleted already, just proceed as you would with any main course. However, even the best filleting can leave tiny bones behind, so go carefully and slowly.

If you do find you have a bone in your mouth, it is perfectly acceptable to retrieve it using your thumb and index finger; once recovered, the bone should be placed on the side of your plate.

Not choosing fish because you're worried about the bones is a shame – you could be missing one of nature's finest foods. If you want to eat whole fish but lack the practice, try starting with a piece of skate. A close relative of the shark, skate doesn't have bones but a sort of gelatinous frame. As skate is very easy to negotiate, it is, in a way, a very good 'training' fish and an ideal choice to start children with, especially as they generally like it.

Once cooked, just draw the flesh off the wing from the thick end down towards the thin end with your knife. You should clearly see the thin gelatinous finger-like 'bones'. When you have finished one side, gently turn the wing over and remove the fish from the other side in the same way.

In the case of flat fish, it is quite simple to lift the skin off; it's a good idea to do this before you start because the skin of most fish is not pleasant to eat. Gently hold the fish with your fork and lift the skin away from the flesh with your knife. It is quite easy now to draw the fish away from the bones without disturbing them too much.

You don't have to take the head off whole fish to eat it. However, if you really can't bear the thought of a fish eye looking up at you from the plate, then remove the head before you start. When properly cooked, the flesh comes away from the skeleton very easily (and removing the head doesn't necessarily make it any easier). Another bonus of leaving the head on, especially in the case of a trout, is that you have the opportunity to eat the cheek – just behind the eye – that some say is a real delicacy.

As an example, trout is very straightforward to eat. In the same way as with a flat fish, pick up an edge of skin and pull it off. It might come away in one piece but it often breaks, so keep going until the area of fish between the tail and the head is completely cleaned of skin. Leave the pieces of unwanted skin towards the side of your plate but not on the very edge. With the flesh now visible and with the tip of your knife against the backbone, slit the fish from head to tail. It is now easy to lift off pieces of fish; the bones shouldn't come away with the flesh but this can happen, so again proceed with care. Having eaten one side, gently turn the fish over and repeat as before.

A kipper is easy to eat providing it has been placed on the plate the right way up in the first place. The skin should be facing up.

With the head towards you, lift the skin from one half of the kipper by running your knife along the edge, and fold the skin back. This exposes the flesh on top of the bones; it is now easy to remove pieces of fish without touching the bones, leaving them in place. When you have finished this side, turn the kipper round so that the tail is towards you and repeat the process.

Lemon juice is a must-have addition to some fish. If you have a piece of lemon on your plate and want to use it, hold it in one hand and, with your main course fork held in the other, push the tines into the lemon and squeeze gently, twisting the fork. The juice will pour out but take care because so will the pips. Do this lemon squeezing low over the plate to avoid the risk of showering your neighbours. Sometimes lemon pieces are wrapped in tiny muslin bags – I find it difficult to get enough juice through the cotton but its presence does reduce splashing; in this case, simply pick up the lemon with your fingers and squeeze it without using your fork.

the fish knife

Because fish doesn't have to be cut in the same way as meat, a fish knife doesn't have a sharp edge. Often very decorative pieces of cutlery, fish knives are seldom seen these days in everyday general use. The knife has a broader blade than a regular main course knife. The broader blade allows the user to slip the blade between the flesh and the bones and lift off pieces of fish in much the same way as using a cake slice. The pointed end and the curved back may also be used to draw flesh away from the bones. The correct fish knife grip (see illustration on page 72) is different from the main course knife grip. It must be stressed that this grip is only correct for a fish knife; a main course knife should not be held like this to eat fish. Traditionally, a fish fork would be set with the knife and was also slightly wider than a regular main course fork.

fruit

At a formal occasion you may be offered a piece of fresh fruit for dessert. You will probably have already been given a dessert knife and fork. You can peel the fruit first if you wish, then cut it up. To be very polite, use the fork to eat the pieces. Grapes are sometimes served already cut into useful-sized bunches; if not, special scissors may be provided. In the absence of scissors, break off a manageable-sized bunch at a natural junction; do not pull off the grapes individually.

fruits de mer

If you are in any doubt as to the correct pronunciation of this one, say *fwee de mair* and you will be close enough. To some people, this is crustacean heaven – a jumble of lobster, crab, langoustines, prawns, brown shrimps, mussels and other bi-valves, probably a couple of oysters and a handful of winkles, carefully piled on dishes of crushed ice arranged over two tiers. This is one of the times that I would recommend securing the napkin in the collar because things can get rather messy.

In specialist restaurants serving *fruits de mer*, some of the opening and shell cracking will have been done for you by the time it reaches the table, ready for you to pull open and get to the soft edible parts. Crab and lobster claws, for example, will have had the hammer treatment. In case the hammering is insufficient, you will be furnished with a tool kit as well: claw crackers similar to nutcrackers but shaped like a small lobster, a long skewer and a little twisted piece of wire to relieve winkles of their shells.

Lift what you like from the platter onto your plate a piece at a time, so as to leave the remaining items cooling on the ice. Using your fingers and/or the tools provided, crack, break and pull the claws and shells apart to expose the edible flesh. You may nibble at the shell pieces and in the case of the smaller crab and lobster legs, crack them open and suck out some of the best-tasting meat. Use the skewer to access the meat in those difficult-to-reach and stubborn crevices.

Prawns and shrimps are easy to peel – they break naturally just behind the head. It's then just a case of removing the hard armour plating, the legs, and often millions of tiny eggs, to reveal the recognisable edible flesh. No one would bat an eyelid to see you, bib in place, sitting up and a little over your plate with both hands at your mouth, eating pieces of lobster.

You may be given some bread and butter with this course and I can recommend a Chablis (shab-lee) or Muscadet (moose-ka-day) as perfect accompanying wines.

If you ever order a lobster on its own, it will have been cut lengthways so that you can eat it from the inside. It is permissible in this case to hold onto the shell with one hand and use a fork to eat the meat.

japanese pufferfish

Also known as blowfish, globefish and balloonfish, this water baby is seriously dangerous food – eating the wrong bits of the pufferfish can lead to death through paralysis of the respiratory muscles, caused by tetraodon poisoning. My advice is: forget it, just eat the noodles.

mussels

No tools are required for this course. Pick up the shell and break off the empty side, then use it as a miniature shovel to push the fish off its shell and straight into your mouth. You can also use a complete shell – that is, a shell with the two sides still fixed together – it will spring a bit on its hinge, so you can use it like pincers to pick up a mussel at a time.

oysters

Once a staple in the diet of the poor and costing a penny a piece, the best way to enjoy an oyster is raw. In spite of metric Europe, oysters are still ordered as a plate of six or twelve; in France you will see them offered as 'les six' or 'les douze'.

They will be served on a dish of ice, possibly decorated with seaweed and some lemons, with the cut side up, pushed into the ice. You might be offered shallot vinegar, cayenne pepper and Tabasco sauce to accompany them. The oysters will have been opened for you already – or as the Americans would say, 'shucked' – and will be lying in the deep side of their shells. They will have been freed from the shell by having had the connecting filament severed. The oyster at this point is still alive; you can prove this by squeezing a few drops of lemon juice into the oyster and see it make a slight wrinkling, shuddering movement.

Some people maintain that the only way to eat an oyster is with cayenne pepper. Personally, I prefer to eat them with lemon juice, while standing up with a pint of Guinness at the races! No doubt you will find your own favourite way to enjoy them if you persevere.

Love them or hate oysters, this is how to eat them. Pick up the shell by the narrow end and support it from underneath with your other fingers. Hold the wide part of the shell to your mouth (level so as not to lose any liquor) and, by slightly lifting your chin, simply 'drink' the oyster from its shell, then place the empty shell back on the ice. This is the only way to do it.

Now there is the question as to whether or not you should chew oysters or just swallow them. Some people argue that the texture of these molluscs is so disgusting they should be swallowed immediately, but I think a gentle chew is good, to release those wonderful flavours for maximum enjoyment.

If you want to appear knowledgeable about oysters, there are two types. Those with very deep pockets would go for our British 'natives' – *Ostrea edulis*; they could be Royal Whitstables or Pyefleets from Colchester and have a flat and rounded shell. The second choice, and the variety that you will see for sale in supermarkets and in oyster bars, notably in Harrods Food Hall, is the Portuguese or Pacific oyster – *Crassostrea angulata* or *Crassostrea gigas*; these are the ones with beautiful, frilly shells.

To 'shuck' oysters, hold them in a tea towel with the flat side up. Insert the point of a robust knife between the shells and, with a sharp turn of the blade, prise the two pieces apart. Be careful to avoid damaging the rather fragile shell edges, and to preserve the liquor. If you watch a professional – in France, a *maître écailler* – he will wear thick leather gloves just in case the knife slips and because the shells are very sharp.

Serve oysters with brown bread and butter and a glass of Muscadet or Champagne and, just in case you've got an aficionado coming to dinner, have a bottle or three of Guinness chilling in the fridge.

flashing blue lights

Although not quite as dangerous as the pufferfish, a bad oyster can get close. Be warned, if you do have the misfortune to eat a bad oyster you will know about it, believe me. I can definitely vouch for this, which is one good reason not to just swallow it. If the oyster somehow 'zings' on the tongue, an effect that would seem to be a natural warning, or you just don't like the look of it, don't eat it. Gently return it to its shell and place it on your plate, then take another. Oyster poisoning is so vicious that it will make you feel as if you are teetering on the verge of death, and will unleash a storm of devastating nausea, the like of which you will probably (and hopefully) never have experienced before. Quite honestly, the only way to describe the after-effects of oyster poisoning rhymes with 'shucked'!

But don't let this put you off because bad oysters are thankfully few and far between, and far be it from me to incur the wrath of the oyster-growing industry by recommending total abstinence for fear of the odd belligerent mollusc.

I really ought to give a mention at this point to those kind people in the shellfish poisoning department of

St Malo hospital – they'd obviously seen the symptoms before. So much for the aphrodisiac of aphrodisiacs!

peas

Unless you are eating mushy peas with cod and chips, peas are difficult to deal with. As I have already said, you should never turn your fork over to the shovel position to use like a spoon, so use other food on your plate to stick the peas to, or squash them together in a group onto your fork with your knife.

pizza

Funny how the best pizzas are never eaten in Italy. Just pick up a cut segment at a time with one hand and support it from underneath with the other hand; eat it from the point first.

Drink Peroni beer or a glass of Valpolicella, or a cold bottle of Pepsi. In most restaurants, it is perfectly acceptable to pick up pizza with your fingers; however, if it seems this is a definite no-no, just use a knife and fork.

spaghetti

Over the years, I have seen spaghetti eaten in all manner of different ways, and I have also seen someone with their head in a bowl of it, presumably passed out!

There are a couple of ways of eating spaghetti that would seem to be appropriate; the first I have seen practised in Rome, so I suppose it's the way to do it here, or at least definitely the way to do it when in Rome. Anyway, with your main course fork held in your knife hand and with a soup spoon grip, dip the fork into the pile of spaghetti and pick up some noodles. Then lift the noodles above the plate or dish to disentangle them from the rest, and quickly turn the fork points-down onto the edge of the plate. Immediately rotate the fork by twirling it between your index finger and your thumb to create a sort of miniature nest of spaghetti.

Leaning forward and a little over the plate, quickly get the fork of noodles into your mouth before the nest has a chance to unravel.

Don't be tempted to suck any noodle stragglers through your closed lips, as the sauce has a habit of flying off as the last end of spaghetti disappears out of sight with a sort of slurp. This is, of course, considered a little rude, if not somewhat childish.

The other way of eating spaghetti is to hold a spoon in the other hand and use it as a platform upon which to perform the twirling. When a nest is made, lift it and convey it to the mouth, with the fork still in contact with the spoon until the last moment before putting the loaded fork into the mouth.

SPILLAGES

If you spill red wine on a tablecloth or on clothing, it can be lifted almost magically by thoroughly neutralising it with white wine; it's probably best to remove the garment before doing this and to take the cloth off the table.

If there isn't any white wine to hand, use cold water. If wine is spilt on a carpet, grab the nearest absorbent material to hand, even if it's a copy of that day's newspaper or kitchen paper, because it is better to soak up as much as possible as quickly as possible; rubbing with a cloth makes things worse and spreads the stain further. Alternatively, use a proprietary stain remover suitable for the fabric affected. It is an old wives' tale that you should sprinkle salt on red wine stains. In fact, salt should never be used on red wine spillages as it will set the tannin stain permanently.

White wine is not so much of a worry because it tends to leave very little discolouring behind.

MAGNUM FORCE

As boring as it may seem, and much to many people's surprise, to be absolutely correct, you should never hear a Champagne cork 'pop'.

The pressure inside a bottle of Champagne is between 85 and 100 pounds per square inch – a huge amount, roughly equivalent to the pressure in a London double-decker bus tyre. To withstand this pressure, the bottle is generally made of thicker and heavier glass than a normal wine bottle and has a specially designed dimple in the bottom to help take the strain. The pent-up pressure is also, of course, the reason for the cork being held in place with wire. A Champagne cork in free flight can wreak serious damage to both persons and property, so should be avoided at all costs.

Moët & Chandon, the very famous Champagne producer, have recommended the following method as a safe way to open the bottle:

Stand the bottle on a sturdy work surface and start by removing the foil from around the cork – there is usually a foil tab to pull.

Grip the cork with your left hand, as shown below, holding the bottle still and at the same time exerting a slight downward pressure on the cork with your thumb; this hand position will not change until the cork is out.

Using your right hand, bend the small wire ring that is normally folded up against the bottle downwards and

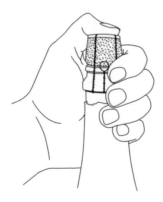

unscrew it to loosen the wire cage from its grip on the cork. Spread this wire wide and away from the bottle; after all, it is now hindering the cork's removal.

With the left hand still in position, thumb on cork top, rotate the bottle with your right hand a little to the left, then a little to the right and repeat until you feel the cork start to rise. You are now in control of the cork's exit – gradually allow it to rise to the top of the bottle. At exactly the moment you feel the cork lessen its hold a little, 'angle' the cork with your left thumb, keeping the cork firmly in contact with the bottle top (see below). Allow the pressure to hiss out of the tiny gap that you have created between the bottle and the cork. Let all of the pressure escape before you move your left hand. The

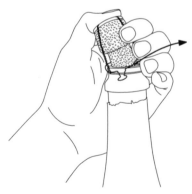

bottle is now open, with no accompanying bang! If the bottle has been shaken, there may be a rush of foam that escapes through the gap.

Practise the same routine for any sparkling wine and any other brew that has its cork wired in place. All instructions may be reversed for left-handed people.

Pour a small amount into the glass and watch as it froths like mad; wait for a moment for the bubbles to subside, then continue to pour. You will find that the frothing is now less volatile, making filling the glass easier and with no risk of a Vesuvius-like eruption. Don't bother to tip the glass over – it doesn't help. Pour only half a glass for each person, as warm Champagne is virtually undrinkable.

Champagne should be served thoroughly cold but not icy and, once opened, the bottle should be left cooling in an ice bucket filled with ice and water. There are good stoppers available if you want to leave the bottle unattended for any length of time.

Don't rule out serving sparkling wine instead of Champagne. A Spanish Cava, for example, can be very good indeed, and the effects are much the same!

IT'S NO CHOKE

In common with other human pursuits and activities, eating is not without its risks. Fortunately for us, we are equipped with a very clever gullet arrangement that automatically opens or shuts to allow air down one route and food and drink down the other; get this mixed up however and things can get a bit tense.

A choking diner is not a pretty sight; in fact, it's quite a terrifying one. Typically the choker grabs at the throat straining and gasping for air, sometimes rapidly turning blue in the process, with the object of the blockage refusing to budge. The person choking by this time is in need of efficient and speedy help. If you have seen the movie *Mrs Doubtfire* and remember the king prawn incident, then you have seen the Heimlich manoeuvre in action. Knowing how to do it can come in handy.

Some years ago, I was called upon to perform a similar dislodging procedure during a butlering assignment in the South of France. A geriatric VIP guest managed to inhale the green olive that was in the cocktail I had just served to her. My first aid course paid off, as my Heimlich jerks caused the olive to resurface with a vengeance and shoot under some flowering shrubs by the pool. The VIP was naturally a bit shaken afterwards but thanked me and said that the whole episode had been a breathtaking experience. The people in Accident and Emergency in Cannes General were very impressed indeed, and the tip given to me by the wheezing survivor when I returned her to the Hotel Carlton was colossal.

From time to time, fish bones can get caught in the throat (as once famously happened to the late Queen Mother). If the bone or bones won't come unstuck by swallowing pieces of bread to scour the throat, your local hospital is your best bet for bone removal. It's probably best to leave the table, especially if the offending item is causing you to utter unpleasant hawking noises and to perform an impression of a cat trying to bring up a fur ball.

CAV-EAT EMPTOR

Anaphylactic shock brought about by a food allergy is a very serious affair. Sufferers are constantly on the lookout for ingredients that could have life-threatening implications for them. Never be shy about asking exactly what a certain dish contains. Even the most vigilant have been known unsuspectingly to eat something from their no-go area. In severe cases, the reaction is so fast that swelling in the mouth and throat can make breathing difficult and bring about a state similar to choking. As this is a chemical phenomenon, using the Heimlich manoeuvre in an effort to help is clearly pointless. If you are with someone this happens to and they really are in trouble, dial 999 as fast as your fingers can fly across your mobile to summon the paramedics.

Fainting happens. It's nature's way of getting someone to lie you down if you pass out. The correct action to take is to lie the person flat on the floor and raise their legs slightly – this allows blood that has been pooling in the legs to flow back in the desired direction. If the person is held upright for too long after fainting, the resulting cerebral oxygen starvation can bring about fit-like movements. If someone faints at the table, his or her head may be in the plate of food, so administer a quick wipe-down before placing them on the floor. Recovery is fairly rapid and a drink of cold water is often all that is needed to perk the fainter up.

Disclaimer This section is not offered as medical advice and the author and publishers accept no liability whatsoever. The Heimlich manoeuvre can be detrimental to internal organs, so use only if trained. A first aid course is recommended.

SOME DON'TS FOR THE TABLE

DON'T say, 'Cor, what a nice spread!'

*

DON'T say *gâteau* – it's all cake, really.

*

DON'T burp or break wind; if you do, it's probably best to say nothing, and if you hear anyone else do it, again say nothing.

*

DON'T blow your nose like a brass instrument, or turn your head aside when using your handkerchief, or sniff – such outright vulgarities should be scrupulously avoided.

*

DON'T allow your offspring to run riot; unruly children annoy other people intensely.

DON'T row over dinner, throw down your napkin and walk out, leaving others behind – it is seriously embarrassing.

*

DON'T indulge in any luvvy-duvvy stuff at the table – it can be nauseating to witness.

*

DON'T apply make-up using a mirror after eating; do it in private, please.

*

DON'T make mobile phone calls or click about on electronic gadgets.

*

DON'T get off your seat to reach something; ask for it to be passed to you.

DRESS CODE

evening dress

The rules relating to formal dress have evolved over time to cover various styles and fashions. In Victorian times, when attending the theatre or dining in the presence of ladies, the gentlemen would always wear formal attire. This consisted of a black evening tailcoat, white gloves, and a top hat: this became known as 'white tie'. Smoking jackets were worn in the privacy of the Gentlemen's Club.

In 1886, at the annual Autumn Ball of New York's Tuxedo Park Club, one flamboyant club member, Mr Griswold Lorillard, broke with tradition when he went dressed in a short black jacket that he had styled on the English smoking jacket. The design was an immediate success, hailed a triumph and subsequently copied by other members and worn to formal Club occasions – the 'Tuxedo' was born.

It was also America that first gave us the white dinner jacket worn in place of the traditional black, epitomised by Humphrey Bogart in the film *Casablanca*. The white jacket is worn these days at summer events and on cruises.

black tie

When an invitation states 'black tie' it means that both the ladies and the gentlemen are expected to wear formal evening dress. The gentlemen should wear a black evening jacket, usually with black satin lapels or other trimmings, and matching black trousers with a black satin braid down the length of the outside seam. However, the smartest evening suit comes in midnight blue. The suit is worn with a white dress shirt, without any frills, with either a wing or standard collar – the collar shape is down to personal preference – and a black bow tie (see how to tie a bow tie on pages 116 and 117).

The cummerbund is a contentious issue and also a question of personal taste; I think it should be avoided altogether and certainly red is not acceptable. Wearing a matching red bow and cummerbund is a big mistake and never wear one with a double-breasted jacket. Comical waistcoats, accessories and bows made from tartan or paisley should be left in a drawer along with anything featuring a *Simpsons'* character.

What a lot of men don't understand about black tie is that it is designed to show off women, not men. The cut and colour should not be messed with so I would advise sticking with the conventional black and white every time. The ensemble should be regarded as a sartorial blank onto which a beautifully groomed and elegant woman can drape herself all evening. To guarantee an uninterrupted smooch round the dance floor, a comfortable pair of black shoes is a must.

white tie

'White tie and tails' is worn to the most glamorous evening parties and very formal evening occasions, such as a state banquet or the State Opening of Parliament. The outfit consists of a black evening tailcoat, black dress trousers with a double braid down the outer seam and a white stiff-fronted shirt with mother-of-pearl (or gold) studs and cufflinks. The bow tie and waistcoat are both white piqué, otherwise known as Marcella, to match the shirtfront. Shoes must be black.

morning dress

Otherwise known as top hat and tails, morning dress is worn by male members of a wedding party, the Groom, Fathers of the Bride and Groom, the Best Man and Ushers.

Morning dress should also be worn at royal garden parties, Trooping the Colour, investitures and other royal and court events, society funerals and memorial services.

A morning suit consists of a black or grey tailcoat, with striped trousers for the black tailcoat and matching grey trousers for the grey coat. These are worn with a plain white shirt, a waistcoat or a vest (a backless waistcoat), and a tie or cravat – a cravat is best with a wing collar. Grey gloves and a black or grey top hat and black shoes complete the outfit. Again, the smartest option is the black but it's obviously a matter of choice.

Royal Ascot

If you are the sort of person who inhabits a 'Ferrero Rocher' world of ambassadorial occasions and hangs out at Royal Ascot, then no doubt you will have made it your business to be fully conversant with the dress code. Royal Ascot is the most prestigious racing event of the season and if you have tickets for the Royal Enclosure, gentlemen are expected to wear black morning dress – absolutely no exceptions are made.

check it out

If you are unsure, and no dress code is specified on the
invitation, always check with the organisers to avoid
embarrassment.

tie philosphy

Face a mirror and follow the diagrams opposite and these
simple instructions.

1 Begin with one end approximately one and a half
   inches below the other and cross it over the front.
2 Take the long end through the centre.
3 Form a loop with the short end, centring it where the
   knot will be.
4 Bring the long end over it.
5 Form a loop with the long end.
6 Push it through the knot behind the front loop.
7 Adjust the ends slowly and tighten.

how to tie a bow tie

Illustration © 2006 Nicholas Clayton
Enterprises. Registered Trade Mark

SOME DON'TS FOR THE TABLE

DON'T push your seat back across polished floors, making an awful noise – just lift your chair.

*

DON'T allow your tongue out to meet your fork before the fork is in your mouth.

*

DON'T draw food off your fork through clenched teeth.

*

DON'T allow your elbows to rest anywhere on the table when you lift your fork to your mouth.

*

DON'T leave a spoon in a coffee cup.

*

DON'T slump; it's better for the stomach if you sit up straight while eating.

DON'T push your empty plate away from you when you have finished; just place your cutlery on your plate and leave it to be collected.

*

DON'T scrape your knife over your fork in mid-air to remove built-up food – this is regarded as seriously gauche.

*

DON'T hold a mug or a cup of tea or coffee with both hands.

*

DON'T arrive late; if you think you could be delayed, phone with an estimated time of arrival.

*

DON'T throw used cocktail sticks, half-eaten canapés or napkins into ashtrays.

THE STORY OF CUTLERY

CUTLERY

a very long history

Knives have been around for thousands of years and some of the earliest must be the ones painstakingly hewn out of flint by Stone Age man. The earliest cutting tools discovered by archaeologists date back to 500,000 BC. One metal knife found dates back to 2000 BC.

Forks on the other hand are not so old but were in use before the year 1000 in the Middle East; some made before 1600, with five tines, still exist. Anglo-Saxon forks have been found but tend to be little more than a skewer, sometimes with two prongs.

The fork came through Europe from Italy's nobility in the eleventh century, having been brought to Europe by a Byzantine Princess (Theodora Dukaina) around the same time. The story goes that the Princess married Dominico Silvio, the Doge of Venice between 1071 and 1084, and brought with her a collection of two-tined golden forks. By 1600 the fork was known in England but was seen as an Italian affectation, while in Italy even the merchant classes were using them.

According to various wills and inventories from the Middle Ages, forks were made of precious materials and mainly for ostentation. Forks also appear in an inventory of silverware taken in Florence in 1361 for Charles V and Charles VI and they show up in Italian cookbooks. Forks were known and used in Spain, certainly by the upper classes, by the time of the Armada. A large assortment was recovered from the wreck of *La Girona*, which sank off the coast of Ireland in 1588; the cutlery found included a large number of forks with two and five tines; the elegant handles had terminals in the form of serpents or human torsos. The earliest fork known to have been made in England is now in the Victoria and Albert Museum. It bears the crests of John Masters, 8th Earl of Rutland and his wife, and bears the London hallmark for 1632.

Spoons have a more recent history; they were probably not really required in prehistoric times but, as man started to cook food, some simple means of removing it from the pot evolved. Very early spoons were probably seashells. The earliest recognisable spoon unearthed is one made of clay dating back to 5000 BC. *Chambers Dictionary of Etymology* suggests the word 'spoon' is derived from Middle Low German, *spon*, a chip of wood or *spatula*, and Old Icelandic, *spann* from Proto-Germanic *spaenuz*.

The wooden spoon has been around for a long time and still has a place in the modern kitchen. Wooden spoons won't mark non-stick pans, are very hygienic and the only thing to use to mix the Christmas pudding. During the First World War, a knife-and-spoon-in-one was developed for use by soldiers – particularly useful for amputees. I saw such a utensil again recently, marketed as a kiwi fruit tool.

metallurgy

Arising out of the Industrial Revolution, steel is a wonder metal; when alloyed with other things, it can exhibit almost magical qualities.

I can remember as a child being fascinated with my late father's tool kit of Second World War, RAF standard-issue spanners designed to tighten up various parts of the legendary Rolls-Royce 'Merlin' engine that was slung in the front of the equally legendary Supermarine Spitfire. These spanners had the word 'molybdenum' stamped across the handles; this was added to the regular steel used to forge such items to enhance the strength and hardiness of the tools.

The first true stainless steel was produced in an electric furnace on 13 August 1913 by Harry Brearley in Sheffield, England; it contained 0.24% carbon and 12.8% chromium. Brearley, working on behalf of an arms manufacturer, was test blending to find an alloy capable of withstanding heat and the effect of the discharge. He came upon the stainless steel mixture during these tests. Until the discovery of the resistant alloy, the problem had been that, after firing, rifle barrel interiors were suffering erosion due to heat and discharge gases. Brearley subjected different metal mixtures to acid etch tests in order to get a closer look at the grain structure and, in doing so, noticed the acid-resistant qualities of this particular alloy. Brearley saw immediately what impact this new material (originally named 'rustless steel') could have generally and how in particular it could revolutionise the cutlery industry.

He had knives made locally by the Mosley Company and it was there that the cutlery manager, Ernest Stuart, first used the words 'stainless steel', having found the metal impossible to stain with vinegar. (The Germans, however, still mark their tools with 'rostfrei' – a lot easier, I'm sure you'll agree, than having to stamp on the unwieldy 'Hartnäckigfleckenwiderstandsfähigstahl'.)

There are thousands, if not millions, of uses for stainless steel; resilient, springy and acid-resistant, stainless steel has a huge role to play in modern dentistry, which, after all, has a very important part to play in the whole subject of eating. Cast chrome-cobalt partial dentures are used to restore depleted dentitions and, of course, in the more noticeable orthodontics. Stainless steel wire is so resilient that, even given specialist pliers, it is an absolute devil to bend; my life in the orthodontics department at London's Royal Dental Hospital was therefore cut very short – I just couldn't get to grips with it!

The most well-known application for stainless steel is for everyday cutlery and kitchenware. The finest cutlery uses specially produced 410 and 420 for knives, and grade 304, commonly known as 18/8 (18% chromium and 8% nickel), for spoons and forks. 410/420 can be tempered and hardened to hold a sharp edge, whereas the more ductile 18/8 is easier to work and therefore more suitable for the processes involved in producing spoons and forks, which are correctly named 'flatware'.

Before the advent of the noble steel, ferrous cutlery was manufactured from carbon steel by master cutlers – craftsmen in the art of sword- and weapon-making.

During a butler assignment one winter at an estate in the South-west of England, I was required to polish the blades of some forty ancient non-stainless steel metal knives after every rustic hunting luncheon and dinner, and so witnessed first-hand why stainless steel revolutionised the cutlery industry. The ancient knives became seriously stained by robust menus of strong game, accompanying sauces and fine English mustards. One very effective way to remove the deep navy blue stains was by using a specially imported German automotive chrome polish combined with good old-fashioned elbow grease. The resulting shine was brilliant, but I wondered if the polish wasn't a little unpalatable? This must have been an absolute chore for the butler years ago and a job more than likely given to the under-butler. Some households had a sort of rotary block that the knives were stuck into; by turning a handle and spinning the block, all the kit was restored to a state of perfection.

argent

The history of the use of silver for cutlery is a very long one. In medieval times, the hosting of great feasts was a perfect opportunity to exhibit one's wealth. Huge quantities of silver plates, bowls and cutlery would be displayed on the vast dining tables.

Silver is an inherently beautiful metal and ideal for fashioning into tableware. It has been in use for over three millennia as the basis for society's economic activity. English 18th-century silversmiths brought the art to its pinnacle; Queen Anne and Georgian silver is still the most prized. The blending of continental Huguenot design with plainer Puritan English styles produced a variety of silverware that has never been surpassed. Hallmarks were introduced in England in 1327; the 'hall' refers to the craft guild headquarters. The medieval guilds tested silver to be sure it was of the required sterling quality; this practice is regarded as the world's first official quality control and consumer protection system. In order to harden silver for making cutlery, it was found that copper was the best base metal to use, and 75 parts copper to 1000 parts silver was the best blend – thus sterling silver contains 925 parts pure silver. Every new item was checked by the Assay Office to guarantee the correct sterling standard and only when it passed could it get its hallmark. Still today, failure to reach the standard results in the piece being destroyed.

No other country in the world has had such a consumer protection system for so long – some 700 years! For this reason British-made silverware is trusted and accepted around the globe. The word 'sterling' possibly comes from a Norman silver coin called a 'steorling' named because of the star design on the obverse side.

epns

Electro-plating cheaper base metals with a thin layer of high-quality noble metal has obvious advantages. For one thing, the finished item is far cheaper than one made from solid noble metal. While it looks almost the same, in the case of silver the plated item looks whiter but it is very durable and the plated layer takes a long time to wear off. It does not, however, really attain that lived-in look that the solid model achieves.

The originators of the commercial electro-plating process were George and Henry Elkington, who by 1830 had patented their invention. In 1868 Queen Victoria allowed much of the family plate to be copied by Elkingtons. Many European royal families followed suit, having many pieces copied. Most cutlery was **e**lectro-**p**lated **n**ickel **s**ilver.

Elkingtons supplied the White Star Line and The Royal Yacht *Britannia* with cutlery. The *Titanic* had the Dubarry pattern which is still available today. As a matter of interest, on every dressing table in First Class there was a complimentary bottle of *parfum* by Creed, now renamed 'Erolfa' and also still available.

and some more hints...

- It's perfectly OK to put your elbows on the table if you are talking to someone across the table.

- Do take a present to a dinner party: a bottle of wine is the minimum, but an inventive gift is always welcome.

- Leave your dog in the car or at home, as not everyone likes dogs around the table.

- Employ a butler for the evening.

CARE OF CUTLERY

scale and polish

The best way to look after real silver cutlery is to keep it in constant use; after a time, the very many minute scratches that form on its surface will scatter the light that falls on it, and enhance the already deep blue-black shine achieved during the finishing and polishing stages of manufacture.

Unused silver will develop a tea-coloured tarnish. Silver is, however, attacked by foods containing sulphur. These sulphur marks can be removed by washing the cutlery in warm, soapy water and, while wet, wiping over with a proprietary silver foam; rinse in clear water then dry with a very clean, non-abrasive, soft cloth. Silver dips are also good for putting the sparkle back into cutlery, but don't spill any on stainless steel or in the sink!

I prefer to use liquid metal polishes, which are applied to the cutlery, then left to dry and finally buffed up with a soft, dry cloth. The polishes do have a rather acrid smell, but the end result is fantastic; after cleaning, rinse well in hand-hot water with washing-up liquid, then dry off with a clean cloth. As well as a soft cloth kept only for silver polishing, butlers kept a narrow, long, soft-haired brush called a chasing brush, which they used to remove dried, powdery polish from the chased work on intricate silver patterns left behind by the cloth.

Of course, stainless steel cutlery is much easier to look after than silverware and, apart from the obvious price difference, it does not require polishing. All cutlery, whether silver or stainless steel, is dishwasher-safe, but nothing really beats hand washing, as dishwashers can leave marks behind and the heat of some wash programmes can loosen the handle cement. If food sticks to cutlery, do not use scouring powders or pads – just leave the cutlery to soak in warm, soapy water.

Store silver cutlery in felt-lined drawers, and place side by side, not in a pile. If you must stack silver plate, put a layer of soft, thin cloth between each piece. A 'tool roll' with individual pockets is another good way to store cutlery and it helps to prevent the items from oxidising.

To avoid leaving fingerprints on polished cutlery when setting a table, never touch the tines of forks, the bowls of spoons or the blades of knives. Pick spoons and forks up by the balance, which is about midway between top and bottom. Hold knives by their handles. When setting the finest tables, butlers traditionally wear white cotton gloves.

To be sure that every piece of cutlery laid on the table is perfectly in line, some butlers use a measuring stick. I often use my thumb and index finger pushed up against the table edge to ensure everything is aligned (below).

aligning cutlery

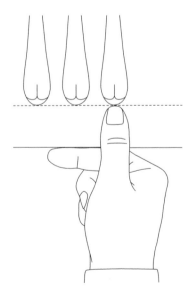

THE LAST PAGE

Eating should be fun and not a time for worrying about which knife and fork to use, and the easiest way to allay those fears is to learn how to eat with style and perfect etiquette.

My hope is that, having read this guide, you will no longer feel intimidated by rows of cutlery and tiers of glasses.

But if you still can't remember everything, or you are suddenly confronted with a new social situation, just watch the host or hostess and follow suit – it's normally a safe bet.

On the other hand, having become an expert on the subject, be the one the others follow!

Bad manners will always be frowned upon and good manners admired.

Displaying and appreciating good manners is not a matter of snobbery.

INDEX

THE NATIONAL TRUST

working to save and protect our coast, countryside, historic buildings and gardens for ever, for everyone

In 1895, Octavia Hill, Hardwick Rawnsley and Robert Hunter, three visionary Victorians, founded the National Trust as an independent charity, to hold and manage in perpetuity for the benefit of the nation, countryside and historic properties in England, Wales and Northern Ireland.

As a consequence, the Trust protects an estate of more than 248,000 hectares of land, some 20,000 vernacular buildings (including almost 200 houses of historical interest), over 200 gardens and landscape parks, and over 700 miles of coastline.

The National Trust aims to sustain local traditions and provide education, enjoyment and a warm welcome to an ever-widening community. Whether you are a member of the Trust, or not, you can contribute directly to the funding of vital conservation work. Please help the National Trust by becoming one of its much valued supporters. There are many ways to support the National Trust, from volunteering and visiting to becoming a member or remembering the Trust in your will.

For more information, please visit www.nationaltrust.org.uk or phone: 0870 458 4000